With special thanks
To Martin Kerr for beautiful book design.
To Helen Exley for believing in my work and your constant wise
counsel throughout this project.
To my husband Jim, for everything.
Dedication: To my daughter, Emily

Published in 2004 by Exley Publications Ltd in Great Britain.
16 Chalk Hill, Watford, Herts WD19 4BG, UK

Published in 2004 by Exley Publications LLC in the USA.
185 Main Street, Spencer, MA 01562, USA

www.helenexleygiftbooks.com

12 11 10 9 8 7 6 5 4 3 2 1

Copyright © Susan Squellati Florence 2004.

The moral right of the author has been asserted.

ISBN 1-86187-729-3

Edited by Helen Exley. Printed in China.

Written and illustrated by Susan Squellati Florence
www.susanflorence.com

Helen Exley Giftbooks cover the most powerful of all human
relationships: love between couples, the bonds within families and
between friends. No expense is spared in making sure that each book
is as thoughtful and meaningful a gift as it is possible to create: good
to give, good to receive. You have the result in your hands. If you
have loved it — tell others! We'd rather put the money into more good
books than spend it on advertising. There is no power on earth like
the word-of-mouth recommendation of friends.

LET HAPPINESS BE YOURS

...a wish for life's greatest gift

WRITTEN & ILLUSTRATED BY

Susan Squellati Florence

A HELEN EXLEY GIFTBOOK

*H*appiness is life's most precious gift. Most of us look for it outside of ourselves. We think it will come to us from someone else, or that we can find it somewhere else. It was a wonderful awakening for me when I realized that I am responsible for my own happiness. It felt good.

This book is about opening to and receiving the happiness that is yours already. You can give yourself the pleasure of doing things you like to do, things that are uniquely satisfying to you, the things that are your passion.

You can give yourself the quiet happiness of spending time alone. You can enjoy... just being.

Happiness can surprise you... in moments of peace and beauty and discovery. Happiness is there for all of us in being close to nature. Happiness is there for you in silence. Happiness comes in thoughts that inspire you and remind you of life's possibilities.

We need happiness. Happiness renews us, lightens our problems and keeps our dreams alive. Being happy lifts our spirits and keeps us healthy.

I hope this little book will help bring you the gift of happiness today and every day.

As you wake up today
open your self quietly
like a flower to the sun,
and be ready to receive
moments of happiness.

Go lightly,
like a butterfly,
and find what fills you...
what enlivens you...
what you love.

Let happiness surprise you,
like a seashell
hidden in the sand,
...a treasure...
waiting to be discovered.

Happiness is yours today
in doing whatever
interests you,
excites you or challenges you.

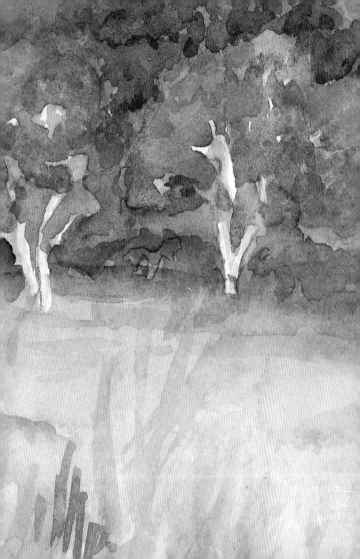

Follow your passion.
It will keep your spirit alive.

Happiness is yours
in thoughts that encourage
and inspire you.
Recognize your strengths
and unique qualities.
Your thoughts can reveal
all that you are
and empower you to become
all you want to be.

Your own good thoughts
will keep you healthy.

Happiness is yours
in all nature...
in fields of wildflowers
and silent deep forests,
in the mystical mountains,
and the song of a distant bird.

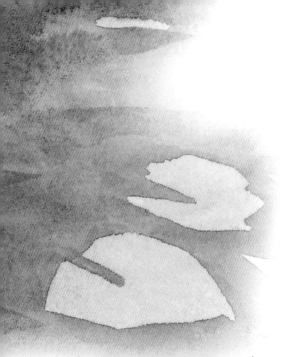

Happiness may be yours right now
...in the park
just over there
The bench is empty by the pond...
Sit.

Be good to yourself.

Give yourself the happiness
of spending time alone...
time to think about
what is inside you,
to listen to the music
that moves you,
to read the books
that inspire you
and the poems
that speak deeply to you.

Give yourself the happiness
of time to just be.

Moments of happiness
make our lives easier.
They remind us of why
we are alive.

*Happiness may surprise you
in the fleeting moment
of a sweet memory.*

Happiness may surprise you
in simple moments
of being there...
to notice the miracle
of a single morning glory
open to the day.

...to watch the dance
of clouds adrift
in a beautiful sky

...to see the reflections
of light and shadows
on the still pond.

Happiness may surprise you
right now...
as you gaze at the butterflies,
so light, so free, so lovely.

Moments of happiness
lighten the difficult times
and ease our worried minds.

Moments of happiness
soothe our soul
and keep our dreams alive.

Give yourself
quiet moments
when the world is loud...
and calm moments
amid the frenzy of the day.

Give yourself
a day of sunshine.
Give yourself the soft touch
of spring rain
upon your face.

Let happiness be yours today
as you find what brings you beauty...
the fresh flowers on your table,
the fragile seashell on your desk.

Let happiness be yours today
as you find what brings you peace...
time alone in the garden,
or walking nearby the sea.

Let happiness be yours today
in finding your own sacred space
where you can honour yourself,
where you can listen
to the voice of your creativity,
and where you can be
made whole
by just being.

In joy, in peace and in beauty...
May happiness be yours.

THE JOURNEYS SERIES

1-86187-420-0

Change... *is a place where new journeys begin*

1-86187-422-7

How wonderful it is...

Having Friends in Our Lives

1-86187-729-3

Let Happiness Be Yours

...a wish for life's greatest gift

1-86187-418-9

On the Gift of A Mother's Love

For my mother from your daughter

a mother too

1-86187-419-7

Take Time Alone

The gift of being with yourself

1-86187-724-2

The Gift of Now

...the simple joy of just being

1-86187-421-9

When You Lose Someone You Love

...a journey through the heart of grief

1-86187-417-0

Your Journey

...a passage through a difficult time

ABOUT THE AUTHOR

The well loved and collected greeting cards of Susan Florence have sold hundreds of millions of copies in the last three decades. Her giftbooks have sold over one and a half million copies.

With gentle words and original paintings, Susan Florence brings her unique style to all of her gift products and her readers have written time and again to thank her for the profound help her books have been to them. People have said that her words speak to them of what they cannot say...
but what they feel.

Susan has created a completely new line of giftbooks called The Journeys Series. With soft, free paintings and simple, sincere words, the Journeys books are gifts of connection, comfort, and inspiration to give those special to us.

As one reader wrote: "Susan Florence's wise and beautiful books have a quiet, healing power about them. What a gift she offers in encouraging us to slow down and deepen our connection to ourselves, our transitions and our closest relationships."

Susan lives with her husband, Jim, in Ojai, California. They have two grown children, Brent and Emily.